BENCHMARK LITERACY™

Grade K

Texts for Close Reading

Table of Contents

Unit 1

Table of Contents

What Lives at the Pond?

A pond has many
living things.
Fish swim in a pond.
A fish is alive.
Turtles are at a pond.
A turtle is alive.
Water lilies are in a pond.
A water lily is alive, too.

4

Helping Animals

People can help animals.
A boy feeds his rabbit.
A girl gives her horse water.
A boy plays with his dog.
A vet helps sick animals get well.
How can you help animals?

Towns Have Many Places

A town has many places.

Families live in homes.

People shop in stores.

Children go to school.

Grown-ups work in buildings.

What do you see in your town?

What Are Some Rules at Home?

by Margaret McNamara

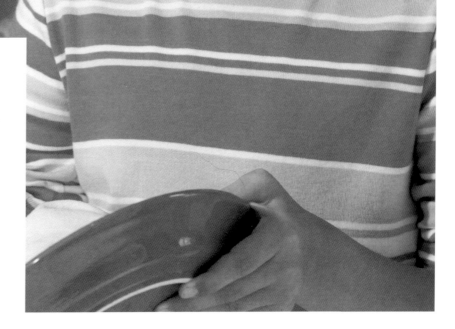

Table of Contents

Words to Think About

citizens

These citizens are members of a community.

healthy

You are healthy when you eat well, sleep, and exercise.

respectful

Helping others shows that you are respectful.

responsibility

Job Chart		For the week of October 20th
Who?	What?	By When?
Miriam	take out all trash	Tuesday evening before bed
Miriam	set the table	5:25 P.M. every night
Josh	empty dishwasher	Tuesday and Thursday after school
Josh	clean the fish tank	Tuesday evening before bed
Lucas	clear table and load dishwasher	after dinner every night
Lucas	empty dishwasher	Monday and Wednesday after school

You learn responsibility when you do your jobs.

rules

These people follow a rule about wearing helmets.

safe

Stopping at the stop sign keeps drivers safe.

Introduction

Rules tell people what they should and shouldn't do. All good **citizens**, or members of a community, follow rules.

How do we learn rules? We start learning them at home. In this book, we'll find out about rules at home.

▲ This family has rules.

Rules That Teach Safety

Parents want their children to be **safe**. They know that children should not use sharp knives. They know that opening a door to strangers can be dangerous.

How can parents protect their children? They can make rules. The rules help children know how to act safely.

▲ Rules about wearing helmets keep children safe.

Rules in Your Home
What other rules keep you safe at home?

▲ This mother helps her child use the knife.

Rules That Teach Responsibility

Most parents make rules to teach **responsibility**. Responsible citizens do the jobs that they are supposed to do.

Parents make rules about doing jobs at home. Parents make rules about doing homework. Children learn that they can get in trouble if they do not follow rules.

Think About It

How does feeding a pet help teach responsibility?

▲ People do many chores, or jobs, at home.

Rules That Teach Respect

Good citizens are **respectful**. When you are respectful, you treat other people well.

Parents make rules to teach respect. Some rules help children learn to share. Some rules teach children to take care of other people's things.

▲ These children are respectful.

LOOK AT TEXT STRUCTURE

Description

The word "good" describes, or gives information about, citizens. Look on more pages to find more words to describe.

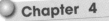

Rules That Teach Healthful Habits

Parents want their children to be **healthy**. They want their children to learn how to care for themselves.

People are healthier when they get enough sleep, eat good foods, and exercise. Parents make rules so children do these things.

Rules in Your Home

What rules do you follow to stay healthy?

▲ Washing your hands can help keep you healthy.

▲ Your body needs sleep to stay healthy.

◀ This family has rules about eating healthful foods.

Conclusion

Good citizens follow the rules. We start learning about rules at home.

Family rules teach us how to be safe, responsible, and respectful. They help us stay healthy, too.

safety

responsibility

respect

healthful habits

Glossary

citizens people who are part of a community

healthy well; not sick

respectful showing care and concern for others

responsibility trustworthiness

rule a guide for what must happen

safe not being hurt

Hickory, Dickory, Dock

Hickory, dickory, dock.

The mouse ran up the clock.

The clock struck one,

The mouse ran down!

Hickory, dickory, dock.

Unit 2

Table of Contents

Stop, Tim!

Tim jumped on the bed.
Mom said, "Stop, Tim.
Do not jump!"

Tim got on his skateboard.
Mom said, "Stop, Tim!"

Tim played his guitar.
"Stop, Tim! Do not play!"
said Mom.

Tim ate pizza. "STOP, STOP, STOP,
Tim!" said Mom.

Mom is eating a cookie.
Tim says, "Stop, Mom!"

Juan Likes to Run

Juan likes to run. Juan runs by himself. He runs with his dog. Juan runs with his dad. He runs with friends.

When does Juan run? Juan runs in the morning. He runs in the afternoon. Juan runs in the evening.

"I like to see you run, Juan," Mom says.

Dinner Disaster

The twins set the table for dinner because Mom is busy. Molly walks to the table with plates.

Polly carries glasses. Molly does not see the dog's toy on the floor. Molly trips! She drops the plates. The plates break. Mom and Polly rush over to Molly. Molly is not hurt.

The Three Little Pigs

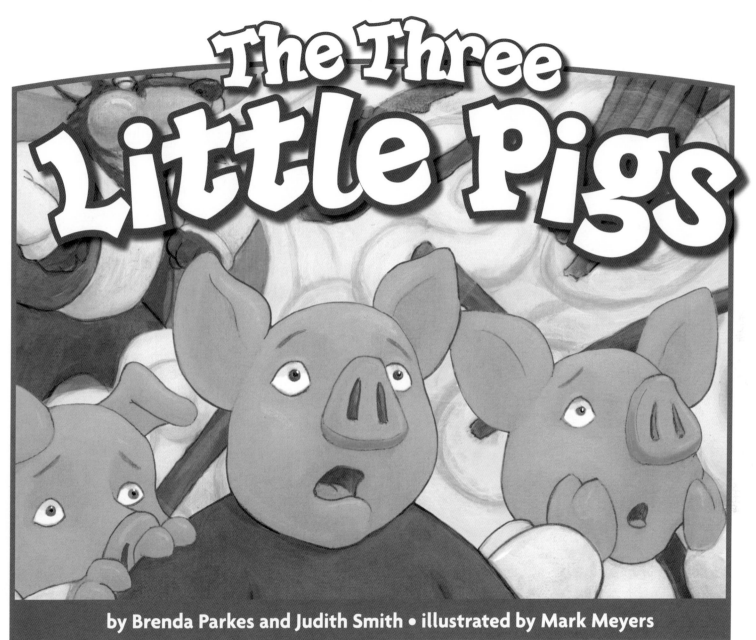

by Brenda Parkes and Judith Smith • illustrated by Mark Meyers

Once upon a time,
there were three little pigs.
They lived with their mother.

The first pig built his house of straw.

The second pig built
his house of sticks.

One day the mother pig said,
"You are big now.
You must build your own houses."

But the third pig wanted
a strong house,
so he built his house of bricks.

One day the first little pig
was making his dinner,
when he heard a knock at the door.
He peeped out of the window.

There, at the door, stood a big bad wolf.

"Little pig, little pig, let me in," said the wolf.

"No! No!" cried the first little pig.
"Not by the hair
on my chinny, chin chin."
"Then I'll huff and I'll puff
and I'll blow your house in,"
said the big bad wolf.

So the wolf huffed
and he puffed
and he blew the house in.

The first little pig ran
to his brother's house.
He ran inside and slammed the door.

Then the wolf knocked at the door
of the second little pig's house.
"Little pig, little pig, let me in,"
said the wolf.

"No! No!" cried the second little pig.
"Not by the hair
on my chinny, chin chin."
"Then I'll huff and I'll puff
and I'll blow your house in,"
said the big bad wolf.

So the wolf huffed
and he puffed
and he blew the house in.

The two little pigs ran
to their brother's house.
They ran inside and slammed the door.

Then the wolf knocked at the door of the third little pig's house.
"Little pig, little pig, let me in," said the wolf.

"No! No!" cried the third little pig.
"Not by the hair
on my chinny, chin chin."
"Then I'll huff and I'll puff
and I'll blow your house in,"
said the big bad wolf.

So the wolf huffed
and he puffed
and he puffed
and he huffed.
But he **couldn't** blow the house in!

All was quiet.

THUMP!

"He's gone,"
whispered the first little pig.

Just then, the three little pigs heard
a bump
and a thump.
Something was scraping
the side of the house!

28

So the three little pigs looked out of the window.

There was the big bad wolf.
He was climbing up a ladder.
"He's coming!"
shouted the second little pig.

"Quick!" yelled the third little pig.
"I've got a pot of boiling water.
Let's put it under the chimney."

The three little pigs got the pot,
and they put it under the chimney.

"Look!" said the first little pig.
"I can see his foot!"

"Look!" said the second little pig.
"I can see his body!"

"Look!" said the third little pig. "Here he comes!"

The big bad wolf fell into the pot.

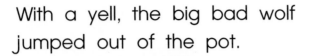

With a yell, the big bad wolf
jumped out of the pot.

He ran out of the door and

down
the
road,
far
far
away.

32

The three little pigs never saw
the big bad wolf again.
And they lived happily ever after.

What happened in the story?

Row, Row, Row Your Boat

Row, row, row your boat

Gently down the stream.

Merrily, merrily, merrily, merrily,

Life is but a dream.

Unit 3

Table of Contents

My Tomato Plant

First, I plant the seeds.

Next, I water the seeds.

Then the sun comes out.

Look! Now I have tomatoes.

From Seed to Vegetable

Vegetables grow from seeds. First, put a seed in soil. Cover the seed.

Next, give the seed water. Let the sun warm the seed.

Soon the seed grows roots and a stem.

Then the stem grows leaves and flowers.

Finally, a vegetable grows.

Making a Bird Feeder

Do you want to see birds? Make a bird feeder!

1 First, get a pinecone and string.

2 Next, put string on the pinecone.

3 Then put peanut butter on the pinecone.

4 Last, put seeds on the pinecone.

38

The Life Cycle of a Frog

by Margaret McNamara

Table of Contents

Words to Think About

adult

An adult frog can live out of water.

frog

This frog lives in a pond.

animals

Many animals live on Earth.

life cycle

A frog changes and grows during its life cycle.

eggs

These eggs will become frogs.

tadpole

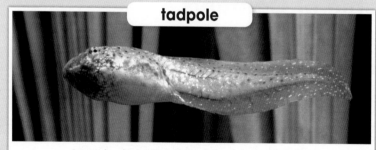

A tadpole will become an adult frog.

Introduction

All **animals** have a **life cycle**. First, animals begin life.

Then, animals change and grow. Finally, animals die.

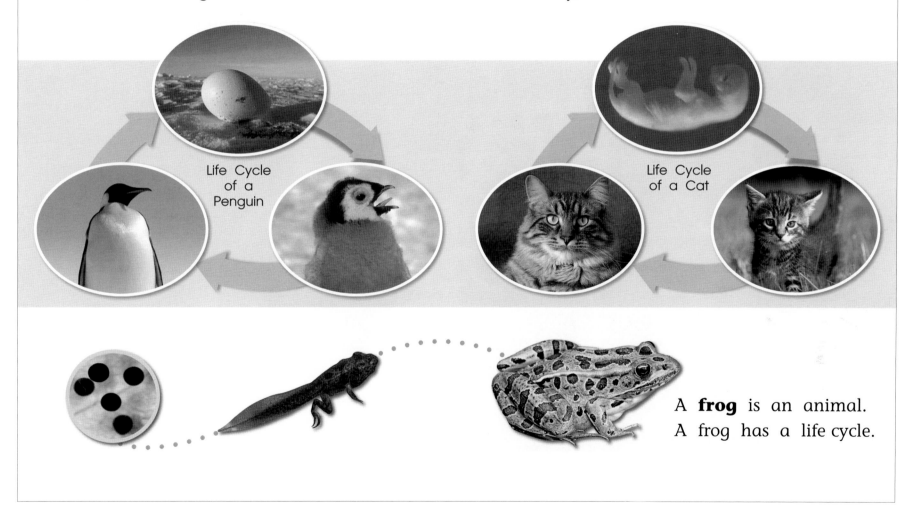

Life Cycle of a Penguin

Life Cycle of a Cat

A **frog** is an animal. A frog has a life cycle.

How Does a Frog Begin?

A frog begins life as a tiny **egg**. The egg is one of many eggs.

After about a week, a **tadpole** hatches from the egg. The tadpole lives in water and has a tail.

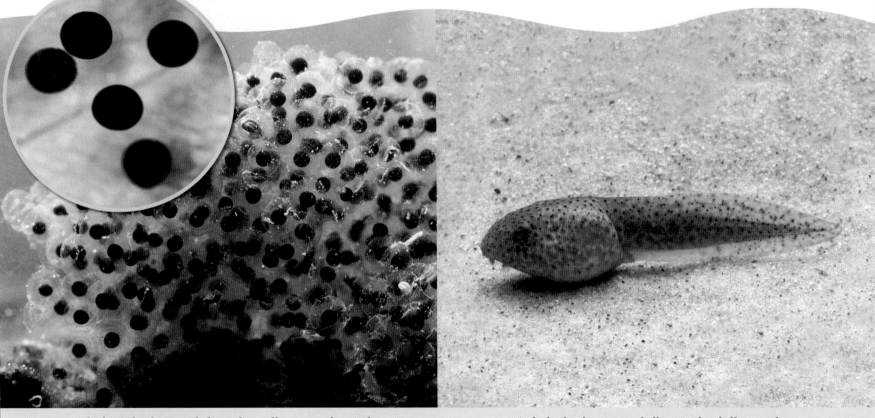

▲ A female leopard frog lays its eggs in water.

▲ A tadpole cannot live out of the water. The tadpole breathes through its gills.

How Does the Tadpole Grow?

After a week or more, the tadpole starts to grow legs. The tadpole slowly loses its tail, too.

▼ Now the leopard frog can live on land.

▲ The back legs start to grow first. Then the front legs grow.

At last, the tail is gone. The legs are fully grown. The tadpole is an **adult** frog.

LOOK AT TEXT STRUCTURE

Sequence of Events

Notice the words "After a week or more." These words help you understand the sequence, or order, of events in a frog's life cycle. What other words help you understand the sequence?

Chapter 3

What Can an Adult Frog Do?

An adult frog can breathe air through its skin and through its lungs.

An adult frog has strong back legs. A frog uses its strong legs to hop, or jump.

Animal Fact

Adult frogs use their lungs to breathe on land. Underwater, frogs breathe through their skin.

▲ An adult frog can live in and out of water.

▲ Frogs use their powerful legs to help them hunt for food.

Each year, some adult frogs lay more eggs. New tadpoles hatch from those eggs.

The new tadpoles will change and grow. Many tadpoles will become adult frogs. Then some adult frogs will lay many eggs and probably live for several years before they die.

Unit 3

Conclusion

A frog is an animal. A frog has a life cycle.

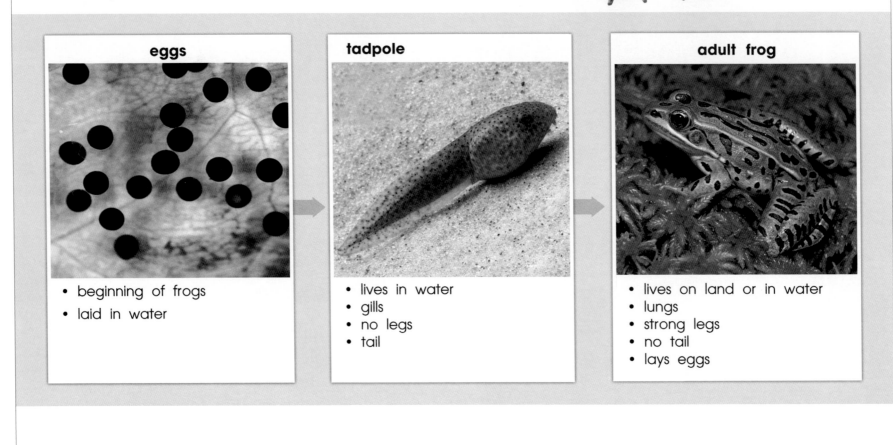

eggs
- beginning of frogs
- laid in water

tadpole
- lives in water
- gills
- no legs
- tail

adult frog
- lives on land or in water
- lungs
- strong legs
- no tail
- lays eggs

Glossary

adult fully grown

animals living things that move around

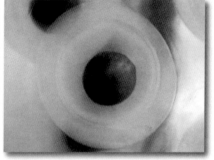

egg the first stage of life for many animals

frog an amphibian that can live in and out of water

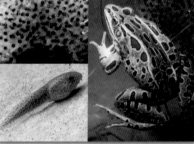

life cycle the order of how a living thing changes as it grows

tadpole a young frog

Humpty Dumpty

Humpty Dumpty sat on a wall;

Humpty Dumpty had a great fall.

All the king's horses

And all the king's men

Couldn't put Humpty together again!

Unit 4

Table of Contents

Sam the Sad Dog

Sam is a sad dog. He wants a home. Rosa is a little girl. She wants a dog.

One day, Sam sees Rosa. Will Rosa take Sam home? Yes! Now Sam is a happy dog.

The Shoe Mix-Up

Megan went to the shoe store with her dad.

"I would like pretty pink shoes," said Megan.

"I would like black shoes," said Megan's dad. The man got shoes for Megan and her dad. At home, Megan looked in her bag. She had black shoes.

Megan's dad looked in his bag. He had pink shoes.

"Oops!" they said. "Let's trade!"

Shoo, Fox, Shoo!

Fox went to the farm.
He wanted to eat Rooster.
"Shoo, Fox, shoo!"
said Cow. "Go away!"
"Shoo, Fox, shoo!"
said Sheep. "Go away!"
"Shoo, Fox, shoo!"
said Pig. "Go away!"

"HELP!" said Rooster.
"I will put Rooster
in the coop!" said
Farmer. "Go away,
Fox, and you CANNOT
eat Rooster!"

52

The Enormous Watermelon

by Brenda Parkes and Judith Smith • illustrated by Mary Davy

One day Old Mother Hubbard
went to the cupboard,
but it was bare.

So she planted a little
watermelon seed
in the garden.

Each day Old Mother Hubbard
looked at the watermelon.
"Grow, little watermelon,"
she said.
**"Grow, big and sweet
and juicy."**
And the watermelon

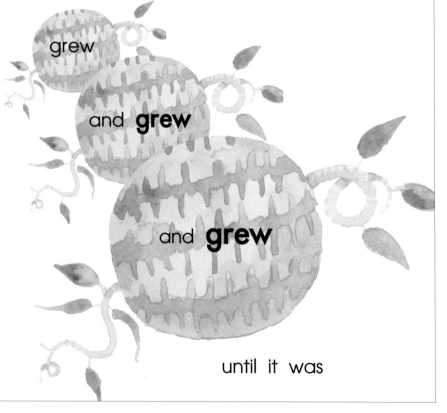

grew

and **grew**

and **grew**

until it was

enormous.

She pulled
and **pulled**
and **pulled**,
but she could **not** pull it home.
So Old Mother Hubbard
called

"It's time to take it home,"
said Old Mother Hubbard.
So she went
to pick the watermelon.

56

Humpty Dumpty to help.

Humpty Dumpty pulled
Old Mother Hubbard.
Old Mother Hubbard pulled
the watermelon.

They pulled
and **pulled**
and **pulled**.
But they could **not** pull
it home.
So Humpty Dumpty called

58

Little Miss Muffet to help.

Little Miss Muffet pulled
Humpty Dumpty.
Humpty Dumpty pulled
Old Mother Hubbard.
Old Mother Hubbard pulled
the watermelon.

Unit 4

They pulled
and **pulled**
and **pulled**,
but they could **not** pull
it home.
So Little Miss Muffet called

60

Jack and Jill to help.

Humpty Dumpty pulled
Old Mother Hubbard.
Old Mother Hubbard pulled
the watermelon.

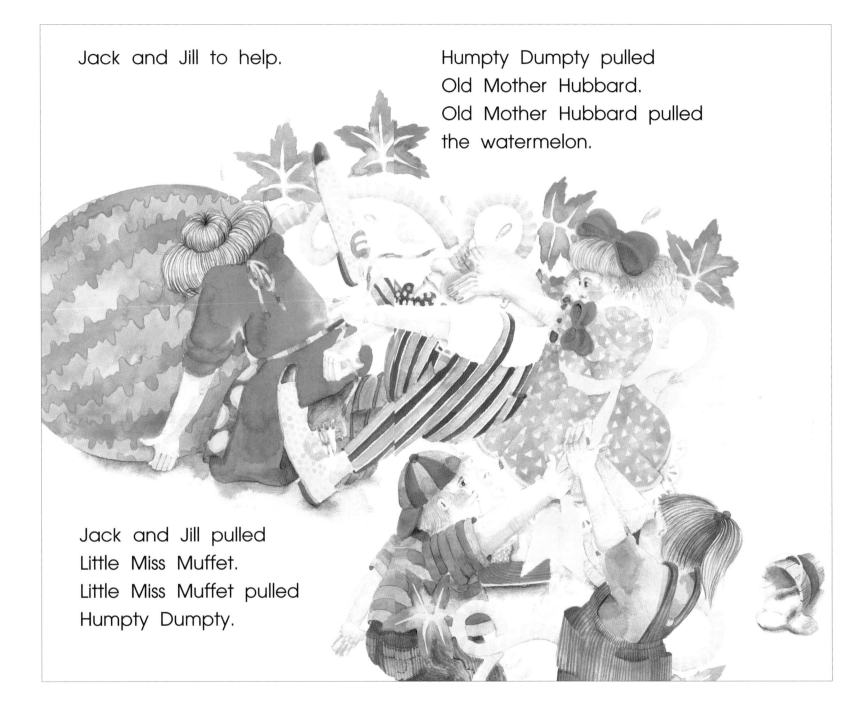

Jack and Jill pulled
Little Miss Muffet.
Little Miss Muffet pulled
Humpty Dumpty.

They pulled
and **pulled**
and **pulled**.

But they could **not** pull
it home.
So Jack and Jill called

Wee Willy Winky to help.

Wee Willy Winky pulled
Jack and Jill.
Jack and Jill pulled
Little Miss Muffet.
Little Miss Muffet pulled
Humpty Dumpty.

Humpty Dumpty pulled
Old Mother Hubbard.
Old Mother Hubbard pulled
the watermelon.

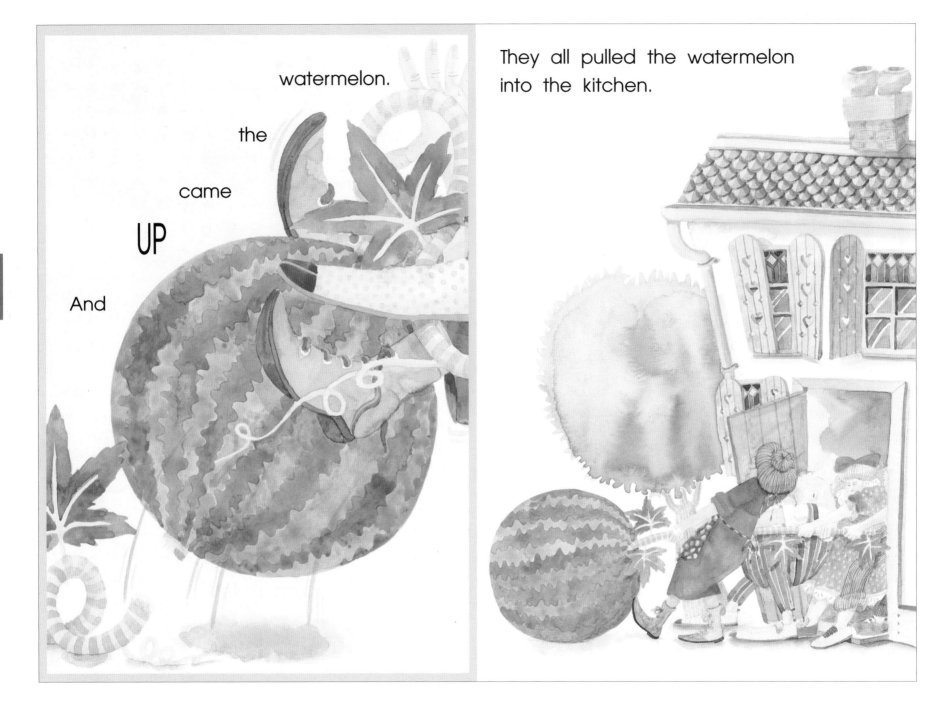

watermelon.

the

came

UP

And

They all pulled the watermelon
into the kitchen.

64

Old Mother Hubbard cut up the watermelon.

Then Old Mother Hubbard
and Humpty Dumpty
and Little Miss Muffet
and Jack and Jill
and Wee Willy Winky
all sat down to eat it.

What happened in the story?

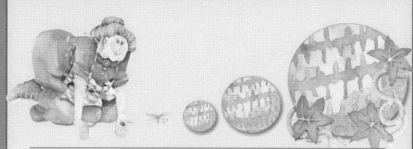

Are You Sleeping, Brother John?*

Are you sleeping,

Are you sleeping,

Brother John?

Brother John?

Morning bells are ringing,

Morning bells are ringing.

Ding, ding, dong.

Ding, ding, dong.

*The French title of the original song is "Frère Jacques."

Unit 5

Table of Contents

Have You Any Wool?

"Do you have some wool?"
said the man.

"Here is one bag full,"
said Black Sheep.

"Do you have some wool?"
said the boy.

"Here are three bags full.
Baa baa!" shouted Black Sheep.
"See you next year!"

Fall in the Forest

Some animals look for food in the fall. These animals put their food in safe places. The animals save food for the winter.

Life on the Farm

A farm can be a fun place.
You can run in the fields on a farm.
A farm has animals to feed and care for.
People work on a farm, too.

Katy's First Day of School

by Tammy Jones and Carrie Smith • illustrated by Janice Bowles

Katy's mom said,
"Time to rise.

Time for school!
Open your eyes."

"I won't like it!" Katy said.   "I am going to stay in bed."

"Please get dressed.
We have to eat.

Think of all the friends
you'll meet."

"I won't like it!" Katy said.   "I am going to stay in bed."

Katy's brother tapped
her head.

"Don't you want to paint?"
he said.

Katy said, "All right. I guess."   Slowly she put on her dress.

Katy ate and grabbed her lunch.

School could be nice was now her hunch.

"Now I love school!"
Katy said.
"Next time I won't
stay in bed."

What Is This Story About?

Use the pictures below
to retell the story.

Five Little Monkeys

Five little monkeys
Jumping on the bed.

One fell off and bumped his head.

Mama called the doctor
And the doctor said,

"No more monkeys
Jumping on the bed!"

Unit 6

Table of Contents

Fun at the Beach

We are at the beach today.

We see the clams.

We see the fish.

We see the birds.

We see the crabs.

We see the seals.

The City

I see the city.

I see many buildings.

I see places where people shop.

Cars drive in and out of the city.

Busy in the Yard

My family is busy in the yard.
We plant flowers with Mom.
Dad gives water to the plants.
My brother rakes leaves.

Animals
in Their Habitats

by Debra Castor

Table of Contents

Words to Think About

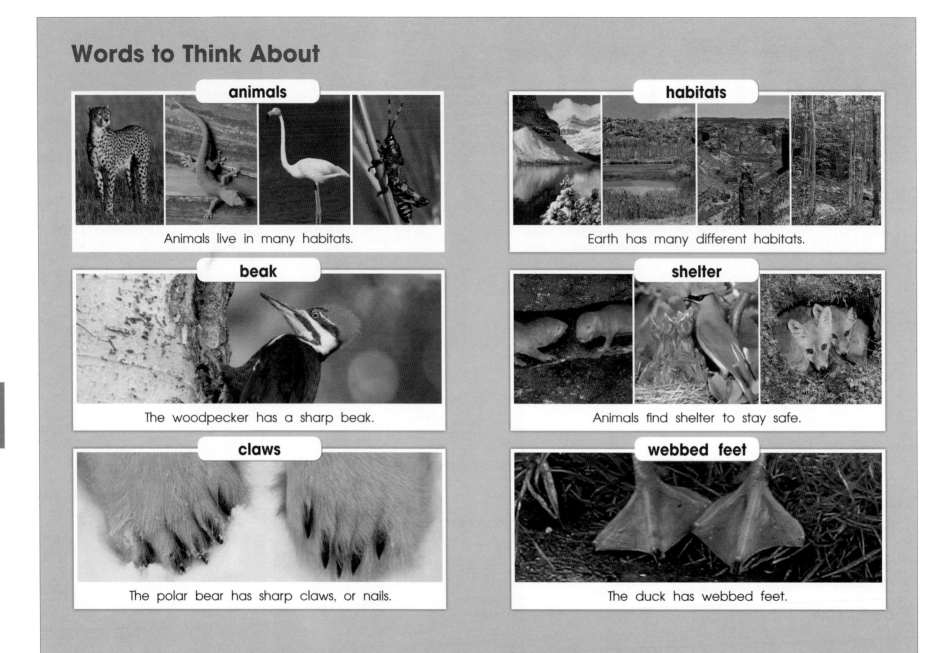

animals

Animals live in many habitats.

habitats

Earth has many different habitats.

beak

The woodpecker has a sharp beak.

shelter

Animals find shelter to stay safe.

claws

The polar bear has sharp claws, or nails.

webbed feet

The duck has webbed feet.

Introduction

Animals live in **habitats** all over the world. Every animal needs air, water, food, **shelter**, and the right temperatures to stay alive.

Some animals have adapted, or changed, to stay alive. This book shows how some animals have adapted to survive in their habitats.

bald eagle

antelope

porcupine

penguins

long neck

long legs

▲ A giraffe survives on a savanna because it can reach food that shorter animals cannot.

©2014 Benchmark Education Company, LLC

Unit 6

Animals Live in Ponds

A pond is a habitat with water. Ducks swim around ponds to get the things they need.

Webbed feet help ducks push through the water faster and swim better. You would be a faster swimmer if you had webbed feet!

▲ Feathers help ducks stay warm in cold water.

Unit 6

Animals Live in Forests

A forest is a habitat with many trees. The woodpecker finds food and shelter in the forest. Woodpeckers use their sharp **beaks** to drill holes into tree trunks.

Then the birds use their long tongues to get food from inside the tree trunk.

long tongue

sharp beak

special feet

Unit 6

LOOK AT TEXT STRUCTURE

Description

The author uses the word "sharp" to describe, or give information about, the woodpecker's beak. What other words does the author use to describe the woodpecker?

▲ Special feet help woodpeckers hold on to trees while they drill holes.

Animals Live in Deserts

Deserts can be hot or cold, but all deserts are dry habitats. Camels live in hot, sandy deserts.

Animals need the right temperatures. Animals that get too hot can die. Camels have long legs to keep their bodies away from the hot sand.

long eyelashes

hump

long legs

Figure It Out

How do long eyelashes protect the camel from sand?

▲ This camel stores fat in its humps. When the camel cannot find food, the body will use the fat as food.

Animals Live in the Arctic

The Arctic is a very cold, windy habitat. Animals that survive in the Arctic have adapted to live on snow and ice.

What happens when people run on ice? They fall! Polar bears have sharp **claws** that help them hold on to ice and hunt for food.

Figure It Out

Arctic hares have white fur. How does white fur help Arctic hares live in the Arctic?

thick fur

fat under the skin

sharp claws

▲ Thick fur and fat keep polar bears warm.

Unit 6

Conclusion

Animals adapt to stay alive in many habitats. The ways in which animals adapt help them get the things they need to survive.

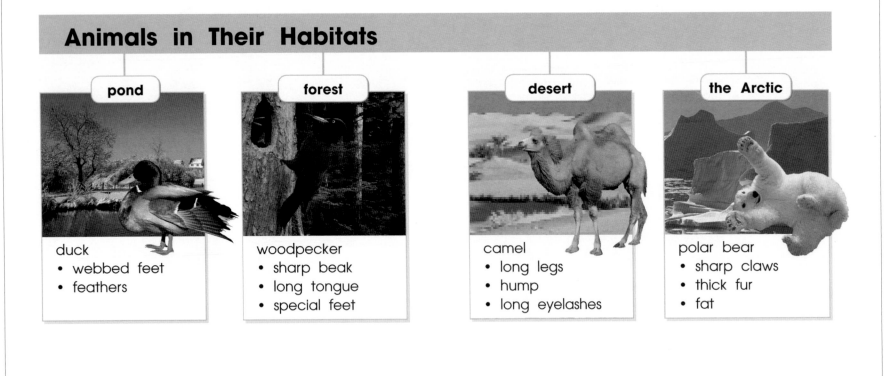

Animals in Their Habitats

pond

duck
- webbed feet
- feathers

forest

woodpecker
- sharp beak
- long tongue
- special feet

desert

camel
- long legs
- hump
- long eyelashes

the Arctic

polar bear
- sharp claws
- thick fur
- fat

Glossary

animals living things that move around

beak the hard mouth of a bird

claws sharp, curved nails on an animal's toes

habitats places where animals and plants live

shelter a safe place

webbed feet feet that have toes connected by skin

©2014 Benchmark Education Company, LLC

Unit 6

Where Has My Little Dog Gone?

Oh where, oh where has my little dog gone?

Oh where, oh where can he be?

With his ears cut short and his tail cut long,

Oh where, oh where can he be?

Unit 7

Table of Contents

Rabbit's Ride

Rabbit is in her balloon. "What will I see?" she wonders. Rabbit sees trees and a lake.

The trees get closer. The lake gets closer, too.

"Oh no!" says Rabbit. SPLASH!

Clouds

Clouds are high in the sky. The clouds are white.

The air gets cold.

The clouds turn dark.

Now the clouds are low in the sky. The sky gets very dark.

Drip! Drop!

Bear's Lunch

A rabbit hides in the snow.
Here comes a bear.
The bear sees the rabbit.
The bear is hungry.
The bear gets closer and closer.
Big paws crunch the snow.
The rabbit jumps up!

WHO'S IN THE SHED?

by Brenda Parkes

illustrated by Ester Kasepuu

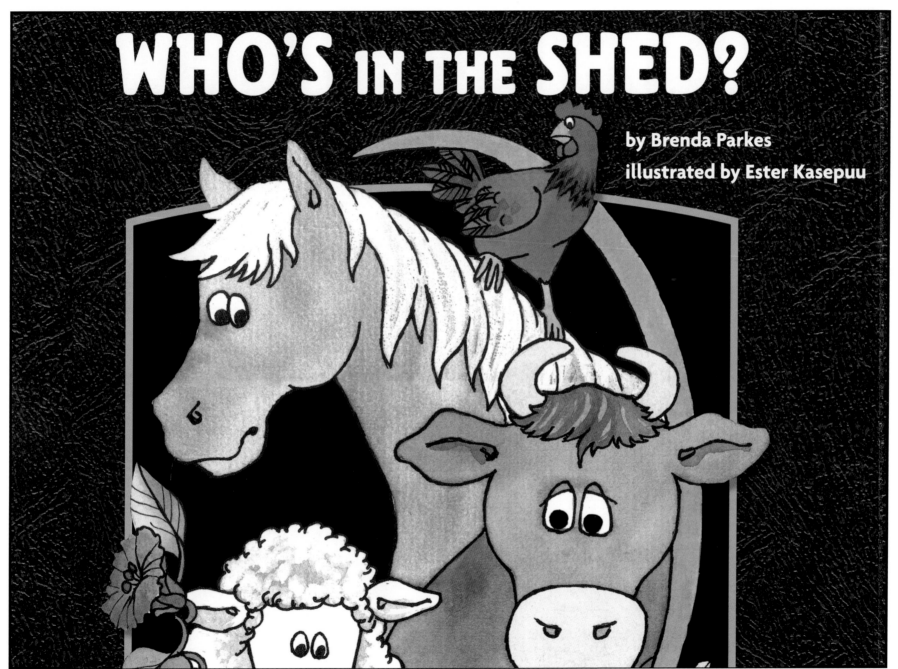

Down at the farm
one Saturday night,
the animals woke
with a **terrible** fright.

as something was led
from a truck
to the shed.

There was **howling**
and **growling**
and **roaring**
and **clawing**

"Who's in the shed?"
everyone said.
"Who's in the shed?"

"**Let me have a peep,**"
baaed the big white sheep.
"**Let me have a peep.**"

So the sheep had a peep
through a hole in the shed.
What did she see?

Unit 7

"My turn now,"
mooed the sleek brown cow.
"My turn now."

So the cow had a peep
through a hole in the shed.
What did she see?

102

"Let me see in there,"
neighed the old gray mare.
"Let me see in there."

So the mare had a peep
through a hole in the shed.
What did she see?

"**What is it then?**"
clucked the little red hen.
"**What is it then?**"

So the hen had a peep
through a hole in the shed.
What did she see?

104

"It's something big,"
grunted the fat pink pig.
"It's something big."

So the pig had a peep
through a hole in the shed.
What did she see?

Unit 7

How DARE you stare!
roared the circus bear.

And everyone ran

away

from

there.

What happened in the story?

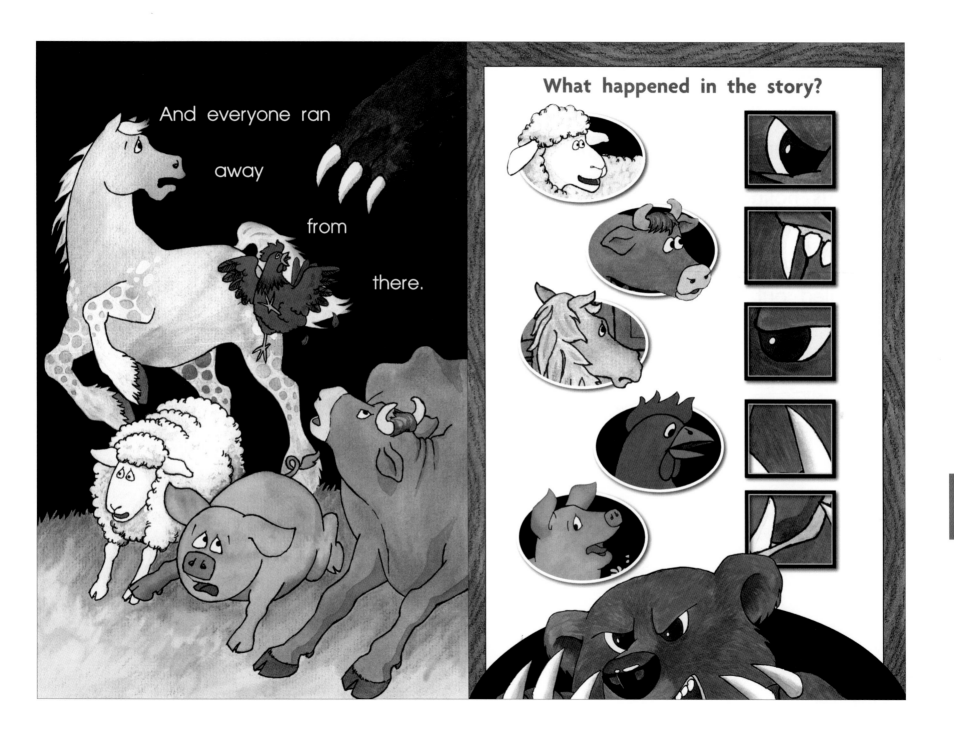

Unit 7

Little Jack Horner

Little Jack Horner sat in a corner

Eating his holiday pie.

He stuck in his thumb

And pulled out a plum

And said, "What a good boy am I!"

Unit 8

Table of Contents

My Dog and My Cat

My dog is black and white.
My cat is black and white, too.
My dog is big, but my cat is little.
I like them both!

What Is Soft? What Is Hard?

Some things are soft. Some things are hard.

A pillow is soft. A teddy bear is soft, too.

A cat has soft fur, but a turtle has a hard shell.

A rock is hard. A key is hard, too.

What is something that is hard? What is something that is soft?

Unit 8

Homes

Homes are alike in some ways. Homes keep people safe. Homes keep people warm, too. People eat at home. People sleep at home, too.

Homes are different in some ways. Some homes are close together, but others are far apart. Some homes are big, while other homes are small.

Children Past and Present

by Matthew Frank

Table of Contents

Unit 8

Words to Think About

clothes

People wear many types of clothes.

future

past

present

future

yesterday

today

tomorrow

Tomorrow is the future. It hasn't happened yet.

past

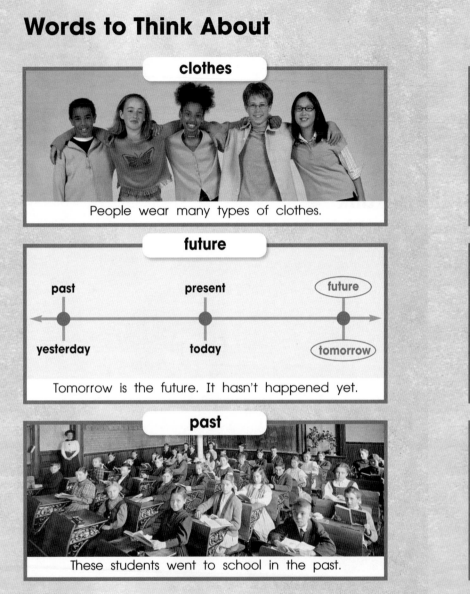

These students went to school in the past.

present

These students go to school in the present.

school

This school had one room.

tools

The calculator and abacus are tools that help with math.

Introduction

What would it have been like to be a child long ago? What games would you have played? What would **school** have been like?

How would your life have been different than it is today? How would it have been the same? This book compares children in the **past** and the **present**.

Unit 8

Toys and Games

Children have always found ways to have fun. In the past, children played with dolls, balls, jump ropes, and other toys. They also played games and sports.

Today children still play games and sports. They still have toys, too. But now many toys use battery power. Many games use computer technology.

▲ Children enjoyed many toys and games in the past.

▲ Today children still enjoy many toys and games.

basketball

scooters

video game

skateboard

Unit 8

Clothes

Hundreds of years ago, most children had only a few **clothes**. Their clothes were made at home. Later, families could shop in stores, but there weren't many choices.

Today families still shop for clothes in stores, but they also shop online. Children have many kinds of clothes—for play, school, and special times.

▲ This girl made her own clothes.

Late 1800s

Girls wore dresses long ago. Little boys wore dresses, too!

▲ Today people can shop online and in stores.

Unit 8

Tools for Learning

Long ago, children had fewer **tools** for learning. They wrote on slates. They used quill pens. They rarely had their own books.

Today most children use books to learn. They also use computers. Computers help children communicate with others and find information.

▲ These children used slates to share their answers.

▲ Many students use computers in school.

abacus

chalkboard

calculator

whiteboard

Schools

In the past, not all children went to school. If they did, they often went to a one-room schoolhouse. Children of many different ages learned together.

Today most children go to school. Some schools are big and others are small. Some children go to school at home.

▲ Students worked together and played together.

▲ These students also work together and play together.

Unit 8

Conclusion

In some ways, your life would have been different if you were a child long ago. In other ways, your life would have been just the same.

What do you think life will be like for children in the **future**?

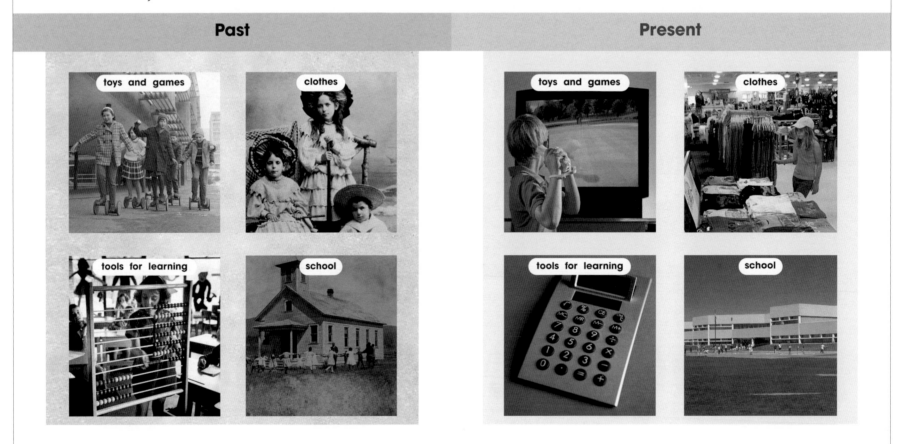

Past	Present
toys and games	toys and games
clothes	clothes
tools for learning	tools for learning
school	school

Unit 8

Glossary

clothes the things people wear to cover their bodies

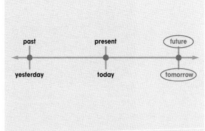

future time that has not yet happened

past time that has already happened

present time that is happening now

school a place where people learn

tools things that help people do work

Unit 8

Little Bo Peep

Little Bo Peep has lost her sheep,

And she does not know where
to find them.

Just leave them alone,

And they will come home,

Wagging their tails behind them.

Unit 9

Table of Contents

The Game

The game was tied. It was Jake's turn at bat. He hit a home run, so his team won the game.

Follow the Rules

We have rules for different reasons. Some rules keep us safe. If you wear a helmet, then you will stay safe on a bicycle. Never swim alone because it is not safe.

Some rules help us get along. We share so everyone has a chance to play.

Why do we follow rules? We want to stay safe and get along with others.

Rainy Day

The clouds are gray today, so we know a storm is coming. Some big storms cause rainy weather.

If strong winds blow, then leaves fall off the trees.

Why is the rain good? Rain helps flowers grow. Rain helps trees grow, too.

Teddy on the Move

by Robert Holl • illustrated by Ian Forss

Teddy is a busy bear.
See him moving
here and there.

Hurry, hurry, Teddy Bear.
Hurry, hurry everywhere.

Unit 9

Teddy wants a snack to eat.
So he looks for
something sweet.

Cupboard's bare. He's out
the door. See him dashing
to the store.

Unit 9

Hurry, hurry, Teddy Bear.
Hurry, hurry everywhere.

Over, under, up, and down ...

Teddy rushes through the town.

Unit 9

Hurry, hurry, Teddy Bear.
Hurry, hurry everywhere.

Teddy zips in for a treat. Then he's out, with snacks to eat.

Up and down, under, over ...

Look out, Teddy! Here comes Rover.

Unit 9

See him running.
He's so quick.

Look out, Teddy! There's a brick!

Teddy was a busy bear.
Now he can't go anywhere!

What Is This Story About?

Use the pictures below to retell the story.

Unit 9

135

Hot Cross Buns

Hot cross buns! Hot cross buns!
One a penny, two a penny,
Hot cross buns!

Hot cross buns! Good for everyone.
All your daughters, all your sons,
Love hot cross buns!

Unit 10

Table of Contents

Off I Go

I'm ready to go to school.
I will need an umbrella. I will
need rain boots. I will need
a raincoat, too.

Water, Water Everywhere

We like to swim in water! We use water to wash our clothes and ourselves. We skate on frozen water. We need to drink water, too!

Look at the Patterns!

Look at these animals. They have stripes! The stripes show patterns.

We can find patterns at the beach, too! I used stickers to make a picture frame. I made a pattern!

The Gingerbread Man

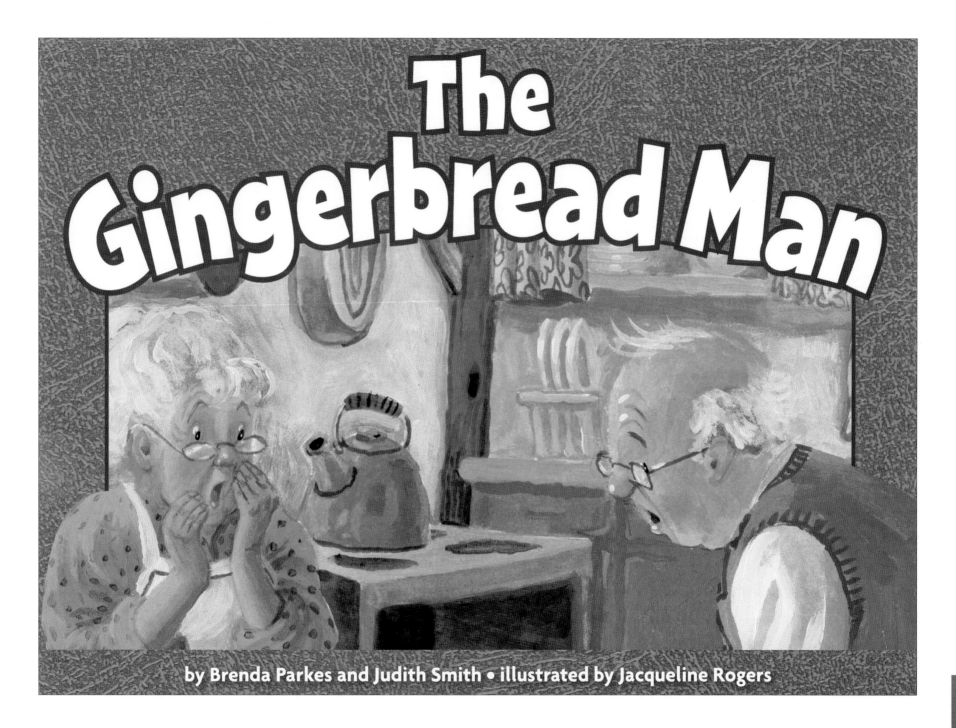

by Brenda Parkes and Judith Smith • illustrated by Jacqueline Rogers

Once upon a time,
there was a little old man
　　and a little old woman.
One day they decided
to bake some gingerbread.

First the little old woman got
some flour and some sugar
some ginger and some butter
　　　　and some milk.

Next she got a bowl
and a spoon
and a cup.
She measured and she mixed.

Then she made a Gingerbread Man.
He had a head and a body,

and two arms

and two legs.

The old woman gave him

2 raisins for his eyes
1 currant for his nose
some peel for his mouth

and 3 cherries for his buttons.

Then the old woman put
the Gingerbread Man
into the oven to bake.

Soon the little old man
and the little old woman
smelled the gingerbread cooking.
"Mmmm," said the little old man.
"That smells good. Is it ready to eat?"
"Soon," said the little old woman.

But the little old man was hungry.
So he opened the oven door.

Out jumped the Gingerbread Man.

He ran through the door and

down

the

steps.

"**Stop!**" cried the little old man.
"**Stop!**" cried the little old woman.
But the Gingerbread Man ran **faster**
and **FASTER**.

146

As he ran, he called,
Run, run, as fast as you can.
You can't catch me,
I'm the Gingerbread Man.
The little old man and woman
both ran after him.

The Gingerbread Man ran
past a boy and a girl.
"**Stop!**" cried the boy.
"**Stop!**" cried the girl.
But the Gingerbread Man ran **faster**
and **FASTER**.

As he ran, he called,
Run, run, as fast as you can.
You can't catch me,
I'm the Gingerbread Man.
The little old man and woman,
the boy and the girl,
all ran after him.

The Gingerbread Man ran past
a dog and a cat.
"**Stop!**" barked the dog.
"**Stop!**" meowed the cat.
But the Gingerbread Man ran **faster**
and **FASTER**.

As he ran, he called,
Run, run, as fast as you can.
You can't catch me,
I'm the Gingerbread Man.
The little old man and woman,
the boy and the girl,
the dog and the cat,
all ran after him.

The Gingerbread Man ran on and on,
past houses and trees.

He ran up hills and he ran down hills.

Until suddenly, he came to a wide river.
"What am I going to do?" he cried.

The little old man and woman,
the boy and the girl,
the cat and the dog,
all came **closer**
and **CLOSER**.

Then along came a fox.
"Don't worry," he said.
"I'll carry you over the river."

"Thank you," said the Gingerbread Man.
And he climbed on to the fox's back.
"Hold on tight," said the fox.
The Gingerbread Man held on tightly.
The fox swam and swam.

Suddenly the Gingerbread Man said,
"Help! My feet are getting wet. I'll melt."

"Climb on to my head," said the fox.

But soon the Gingerbread Man said,
"Help! My body's getting wet. I'll melt."

"Climb out on to my nose," said the fox.
So the Gingerbread Man climbed
out on to the fox's nose.

Unit 10

SNIP

SNAP!

The fox gobbled up
the Gingerbread Man in one bite.

THE END

What happened in the story?

I'm Bringing Home a Baby Bumblebee

I'm bringing home a
baby bumblebee.

Won't my mommy
be so proud of me?

I'm bringing home a
baby bumblebee.

OUCH! It stung me!